Don't Let Anyone Steal Your Story

By

Barry Pearson

Volume 1 in the series *Story and Screenplay Savvy*

Copyright © 2012 by Barry Pearson

My Website, Create Your Screenplay, is at
http://tinyurl.com/barryswebsite

E-mail Barry at barry@barrypearson.com

Cover art by Barry Pearson and Marjorie Lamb

Contents

Some words of caution

The Author is not a lawyer; therefore, nothing in this book should be construed as legal advice. Readers are urged to consult a lawyer for legal advice. The Author assumes no responsibility for any actions taken by readers, whether or not said readers have consulted a lawyer in doing so.

Infringement of copyright

The act of "ripping off" intellectual property settles under a number of names. "Infringement of copyright" is one of those terms, and a good one, because in the real world people rarely steal whole works, the way they steal cell phones or iPads.

In the real world people "steal" a writer's work, his or her literary property, by using all or part of that work without permission or compensation. And this happens in all types of intellectual and artistic endeavors: literature, movies, live theater, television, music, painting, engraving, and various industries across the globe.

In addition, a writer's story can be "stolen" *before* and *after* it is sold.

How *after*? By a devious, or careless *purchase agreement.*

Don't Let Anyone Steal Your Story will help you learn to be knowledgeable and careful as you pick your way through the minefield of negotiation and contracting that faces you.

If your hopes and dreams come true, and a Hollywood producer makes an offer to buy your screenplay, or your freshly minted novel or short story, what do you do then?

You could be particularly vulnerable to "theft" of *pieces* of your potential benefits, like residuals, spinoffs, sequels, and merchandising, so...

You will, of course, retain an entertainment lawyer, before signing anything.

Even if you don't belong to a guild, clauses from a guild's Collective Bargaining Agreement can be used in your *non-guild contract;* therefore, you need to gain an understanding of the guild's applicable clauses. (That's called "not reinventing the wheel.")

Even if you have a lawyer, an agent, and membership in a writers' guild, it will help immensely if you understand the process of a literary property sale. Your knowledge will empower you to give your professional advisors effective direction.

The keystone of a sale of a literary property to movie or television buyers is the Option and Purchase agreement. At the end of the book, there is a boilerplate sample of an O and P Agreement used in one of the Author's sales. Feel free to take it to your lawyer for discussion on how to structure your own O and P Agreement.

The 16th Century precedent

How's this for a story synopsis? When a Prince's father dies and his mother remarries almost immediately, he assumes a guise of madness in order to manipulate the affairs of his kingdom, but ends up killing himself and a spy.

Recognize that one?

It was written around the 12th Century. Its title is *Vita Amlethi*, and its author is Saxo Grammaticus.

So four hundred years later, a scribbler in Elizabethan England flipped the letters of the title around a bit and came out with *Hamlet*. Shakespeare made a practice of building his masterpieces on existing stories like the works of Seneca and the chronicles of Holinshed and Fabyan. Fortunately for him and his contemporaries, everything was in the public domain.

Or, on second thought, maybe not so fortunately because he and his fellow writers had no protection against theft of their works.

Copyright in manuscript

I have corresponded with many writers who believed that copyright is acquired when one registers one's work with the Copyright Office in the country in which you reside.

Not true.

A writer establishes copyright the minute he or she writes words down. A writer remains the owner of the copyright to his or her written works, even if the printed manuscripts have been sold and have never been registered anywhere.

185 countries belong to the United Nations World Intellectual Property Organization, or WIPO which co-ordinates copyright

issues among its members. Most of the world's English-speaking countries belong, and have signed treaties, which means that your creative work is protected almost everywhere in the world, *whether or not you have registered the work.*

Of the larger English speaking countries, only Canada and the U.S. have registries; Australia, India, the United Kingdom, and New Zealand do not.

Here are links to the Copyright offices for these six countries:

Australia, Attorney-General's Department/Intellectual property and copyright:
http://tinyurl.com/AustralianCopyright (Australia does not have a formal registration system.)

Canadian copyright office:
http://tinyurl.com/CanadianCopyright (Canada has an official registration system for copyright, available to non-Canadian citizens.)

U.K. Intellectual Property Office:
http://tinyurl.com/U-K-CopyrightPO (Information about intellectual property. The United Kingdom does not have an official registration system for copyright.)

U.S. copyright office:
http://preview.tinyurl.com/CopyrightOffUS (The U.S. has an official registration system for copyright, available to non-U.S. citizens.)

India has a Governmental copyright registry:
http://tinyurl.com/Copyright-IndiaRegistry (pdf download) that accepts English-language works.

New Zealand Intellectual Property Office:
http://tinyurl.com/CopyrightOFFNZ New Zealand does not have an official registration system for copyright.

How copyright applies to literary property

Using a U.S. example, here's a link to a quick overview of how copyright works: **summary of laws of copyright** http://tinyurl.com/CopyrightLawSummary from Duke University's Rubenstein Library.

Under current U.S. copyright law, rights to unpublished manuscripts belong to the author and his/her heirs during the author's lifetime and for 70 years thereafter, even if the physical property has been sold or given away, unless copyright was specifically transferred to the new owner.

There is a special provision in the act for works created prior to January 1, 1978, but published between then and December 31, 2002. Copyright in such works will not expire before December 31, 2047, or 70 years after the death of the author, whichever is greater.

Works created January 1, 1978 or after are protected by copyright for life of the creator plus 70 years. Corporate authorship is protected for the shorter of 95 years from publication or 120 years from creation.

Works published before January 1, 1923 are in the public domain.

Works published between 1923 and 1963, when published with copyright notice, are protected for 28 years, and this protection could be renewed for 47 years – now extended by 20 years – for a total renewal of 67 years. If *not* so renewed, such works are now in the public domain.

In the U.S., works published in 1923 and renewed will not fall into the public domain until 2019(but in other countries that have a term of 70 years from the author's death, many such works have already entered the public domain.)

Stupidly complicated, isn't it?

Registering your work

Citizens of most countries may officially protect their literary property by registering it with the Canadian or U.S. copyright offices. (You do not need to be a citizen of either of these countries to do so).

To register online for a modest fee go to the U.S. Copyright site: **http://tinyurl.com/CopyrightSiteUS** or the Canadian Copyright site: **http://tinyurl.com/CanadianCopyright**

Copyright law varies from country to country. To find out whether your country has a reciprocal agreement with the U.S., go to U.S Copyright agreements:
http://tinyurl.com/CopyrightAgreementsUS

Major English-speaking countries who are party to copyright agreements with the U.S. are Australia, Canada, India, Ireland, and the United Kingdom.

You can also register your literary work with:
Writers Guild of America **http://tinyurl.com/RegisterWGA**
Writers Guild of Canada Registry **http://tinyurl.com/RegisterWGC**
The Script Vault **http://tinyurl.com/RegisterScriptVault**

The Value of the Public Domain

Some writers only write original works. Others would like to adapt, or put their own spin on, a previously published story. It's almost a Rubik's Cube task to discover whether or not a particular work is in the public domain, unless it was published before January 1, 1923.

The definitive website on searching for works that are in the public domain is law professor Dennis S. Karjala's site Value of the Public Domain: http://tinyurl.com/ValuePublicDomain

Even if you only want to write original works, you might find it crucial to know what works are in the public domain.

Example: You've decided to write a screenplay about the life of Mark Twain. You ask yourself, what published material can I use freely, and what material requires me to restrict my use?

Would you be happy to learn that Mark Twain's Autobiography is in the public domain? Professor Karjala's site has the answer. (It is.)

The film and television business is fond of basing their films on written works. But they are even fonder of basing their films on public domain works like Sherlock Holmes or Mark Twain, because the written story is free.

If you want to write for film there's more than one way to evade paying the high price of acquiring film-rights. If you're short on funds, you have to devise alternatives.

Back in 1975, I was working as a network story editor on a series of dramas for the Canadian Broadcasting Corporation. Filmmaker Peter Rowe pitched us a story about a real event—the 1968 Golden Globe Race, a single-handed round-the-world yacht race. One of the competitors, Donald Crowhurst, faked his position in the race for months, making the world believe that he was sailing around the globe, when in truth he had really just sailed around in circles.

When his trimaran was discovered adrift and abandoned, evidence in his written logs indicated that he had lapsed into insanity, and apparently had jumped off the back of his boat.

It was a good yarn, the network liked it, and they authorized me to get to work helping Rowe put the script together. There was one problem. In researching the story and developing the script, Rowe was using an existing book about the event, and it turned out that the network didn't have sufficient funds in the budget to acquire the rights. What to do? Scuttle the project?

No. Fortunately, the Crowhurst story had been widely reported in the press; therefore, details of Crowhurst's voyage were in the public domain. Rowe and the film's Executive Producer, a lawyer, set about the task of going through the script with a fine tooth comb, making sure that every detail had been reported in the press. Anything that existed solely in the book had to be cut.

To further avoid any charges of breach of copyright, we titled the film *Horse Latitudes* and changed the names of the characters, which in no way diminished its audience. In fact, *Horse Latitudes* went on to win a number of awards at film festivals in France and Canada.

The moral of this anecdote is that you sometimes have to be as creative with your rights-acquisition as with your writing.

What you can, and can't, protect

First of all, you can't protect your title.

In 1987 I produced and co-wrote a TV movie entitled *Covert Action.* At that time there was one other existing production with the same name. Now, the count is four productions and a computer game. Nobody's suing anybody about that.

In 1996 David Cronenberg wrote and directed an award-winning movie called *Crash.* In 2004 Paul Haggis wrote and directed an entirely different award-winning movie called *Crash.* In fact, two novels, a magazine, three television series, and at least five films (not to mention twelve songs, four albums, and several bands) have carried this same title, and no one is suing anyone about that.

But sometimes the fact that titles can't be copyrighted turns out to be a benefit. In the 1970's, a director with whom I later worked named his soon-to-be released movie *Alien Encounter*. At the same time Steven Spielberg and Columbia Pictures were about to release a movie called *Close Encounters of the Third Kind*. Not wanting to risk audience confusion Columbia paid my colleague's distributor a six-figure sum to change their title to *Starship Invasions*.

Many writers who seek advice from me fear that someone will steal their ideas, but—although it's true that ideas are the lifeblood of the writer, *ideas are not copyrightable*. Ideas must be written down to be protected by copyright. And even if written down, other writers may (under specific conditions) be legitimately entitled to use excerpts of your work.

If you are to protect yourself against plagiaristic theft, (and be confident if you need to use the work of others legitimately) you must understand what is theft and what is not.

How does copyright law protect the literary property of writers?

The law in most jurisdictions prohibits anyone from appropriating and publishing the "substance" of your work, unless you have an agreement with the user, or you have given permission to him, her, or it.

Under certain conditions, people can use your work without getting permission. This is an exception called *fair use*. The U.S. Copyright Office site has defined fair use:

"One of the rights accorded to the owner of copyright is the right to reproduce or to authorize others to reproduce the work in copies or phonorecords. This right is subject to certain limitations . . .

"One of the more important limitations is the doctrine of fair use. . .

"Section 107 contains a list of the various purposes for which the reproduction of a particular work may be considered fair, such as criticism, comment, news reporting, teaching, scholarship, and research. Section 107 also sets out four factors to be considered in determining whether or not a particular use is fair:

1. The purpose and character of the use, including whether such use is of commercial nature or is for nonprofit educational purposes

2. The nature of the copyrighted work

3. The amount and substantiality of the portion used in relation to the copyrighted work as a whole

4. The effect of the use upon the potential market for, or value of, the copyrighted work

In specific instances, the distinction between fair use and infringement may be unclear and not easily defined. There is no specific number of words, lines, or notes that may safely be taken without permission.

Also, merely acknowledging the source of the copyrighted material does not substitute for obtaining permission."

The 1961 Report of the Register of Copyrights on the General Revision of the U.S. Copyright Law,
http://preview.tinyurl.com/RevisionCopyrightLawUS,
cites examples of activities that courts have regarded as fair use [I quote]:

"quotation of excerpts in a review or criticism for purposes of illustration or comment;

"quotation of short passages in a scholarly or technical work, for illustration or clarification of the author's observations;

"use in a parody of some of the content of the work parodied;

"summary of an address or article, with brief quotations, in a news report;

"reproduction by a library of a portion of a work to replace part of a damaged copy;

"reproduction by a teacher or student of a small part of a work to illustrate a lesson;

"reproduction of a work in legislative or judicial proceedings or reports;

"incidental and fortuitous reproduction, in a newsreel or broadcast, of a work located in the scene of an event being reported.

"Copyright protects the particular way authors have expressed themselves. It does not extend to any ideas, systems, or factual information conveyed in a work." [Italics mine.]

Notice that, in addition to ideas not being copyrightable, facts are also not protected.

Let's say you wrote a screenplay about the building of the famous cathedral dome in Florence, Italy. In order to create your script, you spent months doing research concerning the dimensions and procedures of how the dome was built.

Then in your screenplay you included extensive dialogue scenes in which the characters debated and talked about these matters. And let's say you sent your screenplay to an employee of a Hollywood studio, which subsequently came out with their own movie about the dome, which used all your hard-earned research, but not your dialogue. The likelihood is that the studio did not infringe your copyright.

As a writer, you should be aware that copyright law protects only the parts of your work that were original with you. If you wrote a book, and you used a widely disseminated source for some of your material, say, newspapers or a newspaper report or other source that other writers could also have had access to, those portions of your work will not likely be protected.

What if another writer attended a party at which someone who had read your script waxed eloquent about your scene in which two lovers meet at the opera house in Milan and make love in a secluded part of the building while Aida is being performed (which is a pivotal scene in your screenplay).

And what if the other writer subsequently writes a scene in his screenplay in which two lovers meet at the opera house in Milan and make love in a secluded part of the building while Aida is being performed?

Do you have a cause of action against the writer? Probably not, because the writer picked up the idea from an oral chain of communication.

In certain instances, a writer can use the exact words used in another work, and not infringe copyright. A writer friend of mine discovered a phrase that had the distinction of being the most-used phrase in movies. As a nod to screenwriters everywhere, he decided to find a place to insert it into his current script, *Eve of Destruction.*

The phrase?

"Let's get the hell outta here!"

Nobody is likely to sue him for that use.

The particular way authors have expressed themselves

This phrase from the U.S. Copyright Office site is an underlying fundamental of copyright protection. In other words, the particular way you express yourself is your shield, your barricade against infringement and theft by others.

If you wrote a story about a boy who attends a private school, likes to wear his baseball cap backwards, has a little sister he's very protective of, and goes AWOL in New York because he lost the equipment for the school's sports team, you might be sued for infringing *The Catcher in the Rye*.

But if the hero is a girl, plays soccer, lives in Chicago, goes to a co-ed school, has an older brother who's mentally challenged, etc., then the particular way you expressed yourself will protect you not only from the wrath of J.D. Salinger's estate, but also from the possibility that others might steal your work. The key is that the substance of the story must have been changed sufficiently so that it is now your original expression.

What passes for "original expression" can be complicated and can be challenged in court. Take the recent brouhaha between J.D. Salinger's estate and John Colting (writing under the pseudonym John David California). Colting published a book in the U.K. entitled *60 Years Later: Coming Through the Rye*, which tells the story of Holden Caulfield in his late 70's escaping from the nursing home where his son has placed him.

This work is original, but after its publication early in 2009, the Salinger estate sued in the U.S. and won an injunction prohibiting publication in the U.S.

This ruling, according to Publishers Weekly, was "the first to extend copyright protection to a single literary character from a lone work." In other words the ruling set a precedent in U.S. copyright law.

In September of 2009, however, Colting's publisher's lawyers succeeded in having the injunction "vacated" by an appeals court that ordered the case to proceed to trial.

As an aside, this judgment may lend strength to the idea that writers can use a single character from another writer's copyrighted work in their own original work. It's a rare possibility that this could happen to a character of yours, but bear in mind that if it did, you might not be able to claim copyright infringement.

In January of 2010, Salinger died, and subsequently, instead of going to trial the two sides kissed and made-up in a settlement that allowed the book to be published everywhere except the U.S. and Canada, but without the title words "*Coming Through the Rye.*"

The whole area of how characters are treated in copyright law is complicated, but otherwise the general rule boils down to the fact that one cannot copyright ideas, but one can copyright the "embodiment" of those ideas.

If you took the seed of your idea from another work, and you don't feel like spending a lot of time in a musty courtroom, you need to transform your written work so that the embodiment of the idea in your writing is unique and unlike the original work

Copyright laws stipulate that one cannot pass off the unique wording of another writer and present it as one's own. Writers have been successfully sued for using a few sentences from another writer's work without crediting the original writer or gaining permission to use said sentences.

I'm about to spin that yarn for you (in my own particular way of expressing myself).

The Martin Amis/ Jacob Epstein episode

In October, 1980, Martin Amis, the British novelist, discovered that New Yorker Jacob Epstein, whose novel *Wild Oats* had just been released in the U.K., had plagiarized parts of Amis's novel *The Rachel Papers*, published seven years earlier.

Some samples:

The Rachel Papers:

1. "My legs started off, at first spastically shooting out in all directions, then coordinating into a groovy shuffle."
2. "I wished she would go. I couldn't feel anything with her there. I wished she would go and let me mourn in peace."
3. "I could feel, gradually playing on my features, a look of queasy hope."

Wild Oats:

1. "Billy started toward her, legs spastically shooting out in all directions at first, then coordinating into a groovy shuffle."
2. "He wished that she would go. He couldn't feel anything with her there. He wished she would go and let him mourn in peace."
3. "He could feel, playing across his face, a look of queasy hope."

Martin Amis's reaction, as quoted by the New York Times: "Epstein wasn't influenced by *The Rachel Papers*, he had it flattened out beside his typewriter."

Jacob Epstein's contrite exoneration of himself: "It is the most awful mistake, which happened because I made notes from various books as I went along and then lost the notebook telling where they came from."

Even if the rest of Epstein's book was totally original, those three excerpts made him guilty of plagiarism. The offending passages were excised from the second printing of *Wild Oats*.

Avatar and the alleged 'Cameron Conspiracy'

Unlike the Amis/Epstein gaffe, which entailed a relatively few lines of word-for-word snatch and grab, the following imbroglio alleges not only copyright infringement but also a deliberate plot in which James Cameron and Lightstorm Entertainment purportedly conspired to extinguish a potential competitor.

Here we have a cautionary tale that every writer should know about, in order to keep his or her work safe from thievery.

On December 8, 2011, Attorney K. Andrew Kent of the Rincon Venture Law Group filed a suit in the Superior Court of the State of California on behalf of Eric Ryder.

In short, the claim alleges that Lightstorm Entertainment and James Cameron, for two years, while working on their project *Avatar*, maintained a development relationship with Ryder on his (very, very similar) movie idea *KRZ.2068*.

The purpose of this behavior, as alleged by the plaintiff, was twofold:

1. to stall *KRZ.2068* from being put into development by any other firm that might compete with *Avatar*, and
2. to make use of Ryder's story ideas and visual materials in the making of their own movie.

From 2000 to 2001, Ryder met with Lightstorm-affiliated executives, visited Lightstorm's offices six times, and worked with a screenwriter who turned in a final screenplay based on *KRZ.2068* in the fall of 2001.

The plaintiff, Ryder, contends that he was not made aware that *Avatar* was in the works already when he entered screenplay development with Lightstorm in late 1999, and that he was not compensated in any way, but that he and Lightstorm had established an "implied-in-fact contract, as shown by their conduct."

In 2002 Lightstorm advised Ryder that *KRZ.2068* would not be made because "no one would go to see an environmentally themed feature length science fiction movie."

Four other hopefuls have sued Lightstorm over *Avatar*, but only Ryder appears to have any chance of success. In January 2013, a Los Angeles Superior Court Judge ordered James Cameron to turn over to Eric Ryder the drafts of Cameron's screenplay for *Avatar*. Stay tuned.

Protect yourself, or 'seller beware'

So what can we take as a caution from this tale, without blaming the victim? Could Ryder have protected himself? If so, how? At the beginning, he had a written work, as well as design illustrations. So there existed materials that demonstrated a "particular way the author expressed himself." He had a shield, so where was the flaw?

In good faith, he entered into development activities with Lightstorm, showing by his behavior, such as fleshing out his story, adding other elements, and meeting with various employees of Lightstorm, that he expected he and Lightstorm would work together to make his story into a motion picture. According to his attorney, Ryder had a contract—an "implied-in-fact" contract.

I'm not a fan of implied-in-fact contracts, having had at least two bad experiences as a result of that ilk of understanding.

Nothing was written down to state the conditions under which Ryder was entering into development of his literary property. Lightstorm went as far as to contract a writer to turn Ryder's property into a movie script. But no contract for Ryder. He trusted Lightstorm.

What's the caution? You can never know everything about what's going on in the bowels of a corporation or any entity that expresses interest in your literary property. You need to flip the old adage "buyer beware," and follow your own policy of "seller beware."

How do you do that?

> Know what you want for yourself. Know what you expect from the other party. Find out what the other party expects. Get it all in writing. Any way you can.

> If you and another party (producer, director, publisher, production company, etc.) are mutually interested in developing your literary property, tell the other party you'd like to have a deal memo.

> First have a discussion about the deal points with other party. For example: You'd want to write the First draft at Guild scale under Guild terms, (even if you're not in the Guild).

> Second, the other party would be expected to undertake the responsibilities of producing, etc., etc.

> Talk it out and make notes. Decide who will write up a rough draft. Write a rough draft together if it's appropriate. Each of you should have a lawyer look over what you've drafted.

If the other party doesn't want to put it in writing— walk away.

The Gold Copyright Blues

When a work makes a lot of money, the risk of plagiarism suits rises dramatically. In the fall of 2011, Chinese/Canadian author Ling Zhang's novel *Gold Mountain Blues* (written in Mandarin) was released in English translation by Penguin Canada.

Film and TV rights were already in the process of being optioned and sold, suggesting that Zhang's book would be profitable.

Because Canadians are so polite, publicity about the similarity of parts of *Gold Mountain Blues* to the works of four Canadian authors simmered rather than boiled. Politeness came to an abrupt halt in December 2011 when a $6-million suit (plus $1 million each in punitive damages) was filed on behalf of three of those authors, Sky Lee, Wayson Choy, and Paul Yee.

Remember the explanation I quoted earlier: "Copyright protects the particular way authors have expressed themselves. It does not extend to any ideas, systems, or factual information conveyed in a work."

Undoubtedly this lawsuit will be subject to much discussion regarding said protection.

An article by Leah McLaren in "Toronto Life" magazine, "Why three prominent Chinese-Canadian writers launched a ten million dollar plagiarism suit against Ling Zhang",
http://tinyurl.com/PlagiarismVsLingZhang
reports these similarities:

1. Paul Yee, *The Bone Collector's Son*. A Chinese houseboy is rescued from white bullies by his white female employer.
2. Wayson Choy, *The Jade Peony*. A disfigured railway worker, who has rescued his boss from death, receives years later a valuable gift from the boss's family after the boss has passed away.

3. Sky Lee, *Disappearing Moon Cafe*. A Chinese worker is saved from a watery grave by a half-Chinese, half-First Nations woman, who nurses him through a fever.

Plagiarism? Or not? Zhang has denied the charges.

It's hard to believe that these events duplicated by Zhang are coincidental, but could they be construed as "ideas," not distinctive enough to be protected? Or is there some source material from which all authors derived their plot events, or could Zhang have derived them from an oral chain of communication?

Tony Wong reported on Toronto.com that May Cheng, a high-profile intellectual property lawyer who represents the three authors, argues the similarities are too strong to ignore. "These are works of fiction with characters and plots that are completely original and unique to these works," says Cheng.

Cheng argues that the appropriation of a work doesn't necessarily have to be a "word by word" scraping of material. The "multiple and numerous uses" of original plot and character lines could also be a violation of copyright, says Cheng.

Why do I include this dust-up here?

Because there are different circumstances in which your work, or the benefits of it, can be "stolen." In the case above, Zhang is at risk of losing at least a part of her revenue from the book in order to resolve a legal claim (not to mention the cost of the attorneys involved).

As a writer, imagine that you were writing a story like Zhang's and that you had actually read the three books. Would you have included in your novel, or screenplay, situations that are as similar to another author's work as those above?

Would it not be a good idea to evade the possibility of litigation whenever possible?

On a positive note, Zhang's publisher, Penguin Canada, issued the following statement:

"For more than a year, Ling Zhang has faced public accusations that her work "plagiarizes" other works about the Chinese immigrant experience in Canada, including The Jade Peony by Wayson Choy, Disappearing Moon Café by Sky Lee, The Concubine's Children by Denise Chong and Tales from Gold Mountain and The Bone Collector's Son by Paul Yee.

"Although Penguin had no reason to believe these accusations, they have been examined in detail and proven false. Gold Mountain Blues does not infringe on any other work, and the accusations of "plagiarism" are baseless and unwarranted. Gold Mountain Blues shares only a few general plot similarities with the other works, and those similarities reflect common events and experiences in the Chinese immigrant community." See the full statement at **http://tinyurl.com/penguinstatement** (.pdf download).

Loose lips sink ships

In World War II, a popular poster with the above rhyme on it in big letters admonished people not to give away information to the enemy. Friends or enemies, it's probably a good idea not to be too forthcoming about your ideas, particularly if you haven't completely committed them to paper.

One of my correspondents had a story idea for a screenplay. He wrote a treatment and registered it with WGA. Shortly afterwards he was chatting with a colleague that he had worked on a couple of projects with, and he mentioned the idea he had.

Fast-forward two years. He learns that the person he shared his idea with now has a TV show under development with a virtually identical premise.

I've been in the movie and television business quite a few years, and I have repeatedly heard versions of this sad story.

My correspondent asked me what the general procedures are for dealing with such an issue. I told him that I understood his feeling of being ripped off, and sympathized with him. I tried to give my writer some comfort and some insight into his situation by sharing the thoughts below.

As we've seen in the summary of the laws of copyright above, there is a distinction made in copyright law between the "idea" and the expression of that idea. To oversimplify, the expression of an idea as written down on paper is protected by copyright, but the thoughts that are in one's mind, or the expression one delivers orally, are not.

If my writer had given his written "short treatment" to the person he had worked with, and the other person had read it and then proceeded to submit that treatment to a network under his own name, and if it were proven that he did, one would have grounds to initiate a claim.

Mentioning one's idea to another person *en passant* is more likely to constitute sharing one's thoughts, and I doubt that those thoughts are copyrightable in and of themselves.

Remember that each person's situation is unique, and it really doesn't matter what my opinion is on any particular case like the one above, because I don't have a J.D. or an LL.B. after my name.

If you find yourself in a situation where you suspect your copyright has been infringed you need to consult a lawyer, explain the circumstances in detail, and get his or her opinion, if for no other reason than to satisfy yourself that you have no recourse.

Legality aside, the person who used the premise that my writer provided orally, although probably not legally bound, ought to have had the ethical courtesy (especially since he and the other writer had worked together in the past) to say to my writer, "I think I could turn out a pretty good pitch based on that idea. Do you mind if I give it a shot?" Then there would have been an opportunity to negotiate a "hands off" agreement, or to allow the other writer to use the premise if he shared a fee and/or a credit.

Making the rounds—and getting stung

If you're an active writer, you'll have manuscripts "making the rounds" or being submitted to literary agents and publishers. If you are a screenwriter, you may be posted on InkTip, Script Shark, or many of the other services that exist.

One writer—let's call him Ben—e-mailed me about a thriller screenplay he had written that made the rounds in Hollywood for about a year. At the end of that time a production company in L.A. phoned him three or four times praising the script, and saying they hoped he and they could work together. That went on for five months after which the calls ceased. Ben phoned them and they said, "We decided to go with another project." Disappointing, but he figured those were the breaks.

Four years later a movie came out with—not the same story, but some eyebrow-raising plot/setting similarities. The kicker was a scene in the movie where the heroine has driven up to the semi-deserted mining town (where it's suddenly snowing, albeit white ash snow) and decides to flee. She reaches her car only to now find it parked at the edge of a supernatural chasm where the road into town once was. A sheriff who had followed her to the town shows up at that point and takes her into custody.

In Ben's screenplay that made the rounds, the scene goes as follows: the heroines wind up at a semi-deserted mining town in the hills where a sudden snowstorm strands them. Creeped out by the town, they decide to flee. When they reach their car, it now sits at the edge of a supernatural chasm where the road into town once was. At that point the sheriff shows up and takes them into custody.

Shades of the Amis/Epstein affair.

Ben has yet to find any connection between the company he dealt with and the company that made the movie.

There are a lot of issues here. Did he sign a release? Have employees of the company he dealt with migrated to other production companies? Is it possible to get a script of the movie and compare?

On the surface, this seems like a blatant infringement, but who's the perp?

Leave a paper trail

I advised Ben that he ought to visit a lawyer and see if he could get the firm to act on his behalf on a contingent basis. I further suggested that he gather all facts and dates, all versions of the story outline, treatment, and draft of the screenplay, all information available about who talked to him on the phone and when, every scrap of paper evidence related to his interaction with the company, and every bit of e-mail related to his script and its submission to the company. I suggested that he search online and see if he could find any relationship to the distributor or the company or personnel that produced the movie.

In a case like this you need to be prepared to provide your attorney with all the ammunition at your command. You could, of course, ask him or her whether the digging would be worth it.

More importantly, when you begin "making the rounds" with your manuscript or your screenplay, keep and create a good paper trail.

I was once involved in a plagiarism suit in which my company at the time had sold (to a large U.S. cable channel) a concept for a series I had helped create. Another producer who had submitted material to the cable channel saw our show and brought a suit against the cable channel, alleging that the channel had infringed their copyright by using their submission to base the show upon.

The cable channel, totally innocent, called us and cried help! We had a chain of title that legally tracked the origin of our production, but there were eerie (coincidental) similarities between the two concepts. We dug up our paper trail and found paper proof of the date at which we had submitted our treatment and (extensive) bible for the series.

The proven date of submission of our series material pre-dated the plaintiff's date of submission. Plaintiff was provided with a copy of our materials. Plaintiff withdrew its suit.

I learned that one of the things a plaintiff needs to prove is that the plagiarizing company, or more particularly, the writers of the infringing script, had access to the original material. The material quoted in the case of the heroines in the mining town seemed to me to be too close to Ben's to be coincidental, so it seems as if somewhere along the line, someone had access and used copyrighted material without permission.

One thing to keep in mind is that if other writers plagiarize your material without the producing company knowing it, those writers have the liability, but if the movie was made and is successful, it's a likely possibility that everyone is marching to court.

A-shopping we will go

As a writer you're part of a chain that leads to a published book, a produced movie, or other entertainment product.

You are the only one in that chain who is an originator. Everybody else is both a buyer and a seller. Your agent "buys" your work from you with his time investment to sell your work to the best buyer. The buyer, be it a publisher or producer, options or purchases the property with cash in order to sell it to readers, or a movie studio or a cable channel, or a television network, or distributor.

There are many different individuals in this buying and selling chain, and some of them pose a threat to you, because if they are incompetent, or careless, or too avaricious, they can make your product more difficult to sell, if not worthless.

Take the example of one of my correspondents. Let's call him Joe.

Joe was up for a rewrite job with a reputable, large production company with a studio deal. In the middle of this, the CEO of the company asked him what else he was working on, and Joe pitched him a story. The CEO said he loved the idea, and wanted the script before anybody else.

When the script was finished, it was sent to the CEO and a few other companies. The CEO hated it, wanted Joe to do a free rewrite to turn it from an R-rated to a G-rated movie. Joe said no, so the CEO asked for a few weeks to test it on four male comic actors who would be suitable for the leading role. Joe agreed, provided that the script would be presented as is, and not pitched as a G-rated film.

Weeks later, he discovered that the CEO had gone to the four actors, pitched the G-rated version, and handed the actors only the first 30 pages.

Next, the CEO moved to a new production company, and took the script to almost every big comedy actor in Hollywood, thereby tagging my writer's screenplay as shopworn goods.

Later, when Joe's agent pitched the script to a few studios, the script was well received, but not picked up.

How do you protect yourself from buyer/seller people turning your creative currency into worthless paper?

What seemed to have happened is that Joe and his agent were moving forward on an oral basis and the CEO took this as *carte blanche* to shop the script anywhere. Try to avoid putting yourself in that situation.

If you want to give your script or book to a person (other than your agent) in order to shop it, get the arrangement in writing. Make it specific. Put a time limit on it. Set out the terms: what amount the person gets paid if a deal is struck, what production involvement the person gets if the project goes into production, what credit, if any, the person gets.

Cover all the bases. Pin everything down and get it in writing. And last, but not least, (you guessed it) consult an attorney.

You've got an offer!

Most writers are concerned about someone stealing their story during the period of time when they are prospecting for buyers, before they are presented with an offer. It might seem that after you have an offer, your worries are over.

Not exactly.

When an offer hits your desk, you are into a different phase of protecting your work. This is the time to ensure that you're getting a fair deal, and that you are protecting the full potential of the manuscript or screenplay you're going to sell.

Writers unfamiliar with the publishing or movie and television business may cast their eyes on the wrong issues.

A writer—let's call her Allison—sought advice from me about an offer she received from a producer who wanted to discuss buying the rights to her about-to-be-published book. Allison's main concern was one that arose from her lack of experience with the movie industry. "I don't mind some changes," she wrote me, "but I would want the script to reflect the book."

It's reasonable for a prose writer to hope that the screenplay would "reflect" the book. It's not reasonable to expect that a producer or production company would only make "some changes."

Authors, be prepared. They're going to make *a lot* of changes.

Ernest Hemingway, who earned a truckload of money selling his works to Hollywood, and mostly hated the movies made from them, had advice for fellow writers. He told them that if they wanted to sell their books to Hollywood, they should go to the California/Nevada state border, throw the book across, then run like hell in the other direction.

J.D. Salinger, author of *The Catcher in the Rye* among several other books and stories, hated the movie business and never allowed anyone to make a movie from any of his works. He believed it would besmirch and degrade his characters and their stories.

So, is selling to Hollywood an issue of how much integrity a writer has? No it's usually an issue of making money, so that you, the writer can afford to keep doing what you love best—writing.

Whether your work is a novel, a short story, an article, an exposé or a screenplay, when the movie makers come knocking, you need to be aware of all the ways they can "steal" your work by negotiating it away from you.

The fidelity that the movie will have to the original work is a reasonable concern, but it's an issue that should be addressed last.

Allison had already taken steps to protect herself from story larceny. She wrote, "I have a registered copyright on the manuscript, and I have required nondisclosure agreements from everyone, but I am not sure what to do once I am officially approached by a funded producer."

Most writers, whether novices or veterans, hope for a first experience of being approached by a potential buyer, be it publisher, producer, production company, network, or studio.

But buyers seldom come prepared with instant funding to produce a movie. First there is a process of development to go through before the buyer would commit to funding. This development period might be one to two years long, and will primarily entail the development of a screenplay and a budget.

The O and P

A serious buyer will likely want to take an option on your literary property in the form of an "Option and Purchase" (O and P) agreement. (There is a sample of such an agreement at the end of this book.)

Now—how do you protect yourself from getting a bad deal?

You hire an entertainment lawyer to help you negotiate the agreement. Don't hire the lawyer who did the closing on your house purchase. Don't hire the lawyer who handled your divorce. Hire a specialist who knows the territory. They are not hard to find, and most of them will be very familiar with handling a standard O and P agreement.

If the buyer doesn't want to have his lawyer deal with your lawyer, run like hell in the other direction.

The typical O and P is composed of two parts: an "Option to Purchase" section, and a "Purchase Agreement" that has been agreed upon and signed by both parties.

The Option to Purchase, in addition to clauses about the option itself, provides the buyer with the right to "exercise" the Purchase Agreement under certain conditions.

The Purchase Agreement containing all the terms of the purchase of your literary work is attached to the Option Agreement. This means that all the purchaser needs to do is to notify you and meet all the conditions of purchase, including pre-agreed payments, and your work is sold.

Under such agreement, the writer (you) would typically be paid an option fee upon signing the agreement, which would tie up the rights to your literary property for a specified period of time (meaning you can't go shopping it around until the Option expires).

As you can see, the O and P Agreement is a reasonably complicated one, which is why you need a lawyer.

You can be flexible on the Option part of the agreement, unless it ties up the property for too long a time for too little option payment.

The Purchase part of the agreement is the one to pay attention to. It's likely that your attorney will battle for the best deal for you, but here are the fundamental things I would be looking for as a writer:

Whether you belong to the Writers Guild or not, look for your fee to be at least Guild scale conditions and payment, as set out in the WGA Schedule of Minimums.
http://tinyurl.com/ScheduleMinimumsWGA

This schedule sets out minimum payment amounts for theatrical and TV stories, treatments, screenplays, and teleplays for various lengths and types of programs.

If the movie is lower budget and you are not a Guild member you may wish to negotiate a set of fees related to a percentage of Guild fees.

Your fee should be completely paid by the first day of principal photography.

All royalty fees [NOT PROFIT-BASED FEES] should be worked out for all spin-offs, sequels, prequels, television series, and ancillaries, including DVD sales, video games derived from the story and characters, toys based on your characters, and novelizations.

If your literary property is a book, the likelihood is that the movie made from your book will generate much more revenue for you than your book (unless you're J.K. Rowling, but she did okay with the movies as well); therefore, you should be prepared for significant changes, omissions, or additions to your story, in order to transform it into a successful movie story.

I recommend you be very flexible in this regard. Many good things can stem from production of a movie from your book. If you are concerned about your reputation, you may wish to reserve the right to remove your name from the credits in the rare event that the finished movie offends you in some way.

The good things? Well, first, the publicity generated by the movie could ramp up your sales of the book significantly. And if the movie is a success, the company may want to make a sequel or a television series from it, all of which should, by your contract, entitle you to very healthy remuneration.

A cautionary note: in the option business, as in the Bible, "Many are called, but few are chosen." My recommendation? Once you have signed your O and P Agreement, forget about it and launch into writing your next book or screenplay, without a backward glance.

Chain of title

The term "chain of title" is used a lot in the process of optioning, or acquiring the rights to a literary property in the movie and television business.

The chain of title is a written, detailed summary and collection of documents that trace the life-story of a literary property from its embryonic inception to the present.

Typically an O and P Agreement will contain a requirement for you to provide a legal "opinion on title." This means that a lawyer will have to attest to the fact that you "hold title" to your work.

Although chain of title is primarily a legal document, it can be a strong protector for you—the creator and writer. So, to prevent anyone from stealing your story at any time, it's a good idea to document the chain of title of your work. Start at the point at which you incubated the idea—something like an Aha! Moment:

"Dec. 21, 2011 (always date your records) I was reading the New York Times, and I came across this article about...."

And then a next entry: "January 5, 2012. This is the page-and-a-half I wrote today about the treatment I'm going to write. I'm thinking of calling it [one or more title possibilities here]."

Writing with a partner

What happens when two people write together? Sometimes it's good, sometimes—not so good.

I have an acquaintance—let's call him Frank—who wrote a story with another writer. Frank reports the collaboration thus:

> "I have written on my own, a screenplay [from the story]; he [Frank's co-writer on the story] says he will eventually write a book based on the story. He is asking for a 50-50 share of profits derived from the eventual selling of book and screenplay. I have offered that we split the story rights 50-50 and each keep the proceeds from our respective platforms (screenplay, book); so far there is no written and signed agreement between us. Am I right to offer only to split story rights? Would I win a court case?"

I responded to Frank thus:

> You don't ever want to go to litigation of any kind, except in dire circumstances. Please don't!

> Your co-story writer may feel this is a fair deal, believing that he will surely finish the novel and get it published. I will tell you from experience, that it is about five times as hard to write a novel as a screenplay; therefore, chances are he will not finish the novel or put it out to a publisher.

> Nevertheless, it would be manifestly unfair for him to refuse to agree to, or sign any agreement with you. That would make your screenplay unmarketable, and if he doesn't sign with you, you may as well put your screenplay in a drawer, or use it as a paperweight.

When a screenplay is produced, the fees are split into story fees, script (screenplay) fees, and production fees.

One can sell the script for a specified fee, but the movie might not get made. Usually the story fees are 20% of the total paid, and the script fees are 80% of said fee.

If the movie is made, there will be a further sum, the production fee, paid on the first day of principal photography, and that amount will be split 20% to the credited storywriters, and 80% to the credited scriptwriters.

In the case of Frank and his co-storywriter, if the Guild terms were applied, the co-storywriter would get 10% of the fee, since he wrote in partnership with Frank. Frank would get 10% + 80% (for the script) = 90%. Although he's not obligated to do so, a more than fair deal would be for Frank to give his co-writer the whole story fee on any sale.

Again, screenplay writers rarely see "profits." If they work under a Guild contract, they will get a buyout for certain uses, and/or residuals for further uses. In a non-union contract the screenwriter will get a negotiated fee, and that's all he or she will ever see.

I suggested to Frank that he talk with the other writer, decide what terms they could mutually agree to, then write those terms up and consult separate lawyers before signing.

I thought he should be aware that perhaps neither of their works would ever sell, especially for huge money, so he ought to be prepared to walk away. If that was the course he took, his co-writer could never use or sell what the two of them had written. I recommended that Frank register the story, not the screenplay, with WGA, citing both of them as the writers. Then he would have some evidence as to when the work was written, and that he was a part of it.

Frank responded that when he suggested his co-writer meet with him to work out an agreement, the co-writer refused.

As this situation unfolded, it turned out that Frank's writing partner, even though the original idea was his, was not writing a book, and probably never would. And as of this writing, the relationship between Frank and his co-writer has ended, and Frank has abandoned the idea of the screenplay, has shelved the project, and has turned to writing books.

How could Frank have protected himself? I suspect that you already have the answer, but I'll let him tell it in his words, "Lesson learned: get a written agreement beforehand."

Here's another anecdote about collaboration. A writer—let's call her Jane—met a female producer who asked if Jane would be interested in writing a TV pilot. Jane went ahead and wrote the pilot, and then the two of them found a buyer who was willing to read the script. So at that point they wanted to write up a contract. Jane, who had done all the writing asked me," What is fair? What needs to be considered and put into the contract?"

In hindsight, as my acquaintance Frank had discovered to his chagrin, Jane probably should have worked out her contract before starting to write. In Jane's case it wasn't too late because she hadn't signed anything, and by committing her idea to written form her script was copyright in manuscript. She owned it. In fact she may have had an advantage in negotiating her deal with her producer.

Since I'm not a lawyer I can't give legal advice, but I could tell her what I look for in my own writer contracts, which usually set out three basic items:

1. The terms and conditions under which I will work.

2. The fee to be paid and the timing of the payments.

3. The credit I will receive.

Other clauses may deal with matters specific to the type of work, or the situation of the contracting parties.

So, in the case of the above TV idea the two collaborators might begin by agreeing on and writing up 1, 2, and 3, plus anything else they can think of.

Under number 1, the terms and conditions, they need to decide whether they'll work together on the stories, and then pass the stories on to selected writers to do the scripts, which is often the case in TV scripting, or if there will be some other arrangement.

Under number 2, the fee, they need to determine how they will split the fee. A typical split in screenplay writing is 20% for the story, 80% for the script.

Under number 3, it would be fair if the producer with the idea got a "Story by" credit, and the writer received a "TV Pilot by" or a "Teleplay by" credit. If you're a WGA writer, the WGA spells out the wording that is acceptable for credits.

In your case, if you are writing with a partner, or collaborating, it would be useful to check out the terms in the WGA agreement (.pdf download),
http://tinyurl.com/AgreementWGA
which you can find on the WGA website and make an agreement between you and your partner before you start to write.

Eventually if you are writing with a partner you will want to offer your work to a third party, possibly a buyer, so you need to decide between you what your roles might be if the buyer accepts your project, and you should put that down in your contract.

You need to consider what happens if one of you abandons the project. Does the other party have the right to carry on to get it produced? What rights would the leaving party retain? What rights would the continuing party have?

I strongly recommend that you consult a lawyer before finalizing and signing anything.

Plagiarism pops up everywhere

Sometimes it's hard to prevent or to punish plagiarism, as evidenced by this story from a twice-bitten writer.

"I have successfully published several well received scientific works... but have been snake-bit with attempting commercial work... one previous screenplay was plagiarized... my agent sent a work [of mine] around to various potential buyers... perhaps 15-20 mailings to supposedly legit people. My agent received some queries and nibbles but nothing concrete...

I was shocked about two years later to find my plot... with its twists and turns... show up on a made-for-TV movie with somewhat different characters...I know you're thinking coincidence... but the plot was fairly original in topic and the twists were mirrored in this blatant plagiarism... not the first time this has happened to me... sent some ideas to a local comedy TV show as part of a resume for a job as a writer... literally days later the ideas/storylines showed up on the TV show... of course I wasn't asked for even an interview... when confronting the host he admitted using my ideas and thought I should be "complimented." I have a feeling this goes on much more often than the public can guess... the screenplay was copyrighted but who needs the headache of a long lawsuit against deep pocket people... is there a logical way for a writer without good/honest leads for his material to avoid the plagiarist/bottom feeders of the industry... I wonder if a number of "professional readers" aren't just fishing for somebody else's ideas... even had an ex-college prof steal a term paper and publish under his slightly re-written version in a literary journal ... and have the gall to thank me in front of grad class for the genesis of his work... genesis... it was my work..."

My reply: I can't help you with the term paper rip-off, but I recommend that you pursue the other infringements of your copyright.

You owe it to yourself and to other unsuspecting writers who follow you.

Infringement of copyright is theft, and carries severe penalties. In many jurisdictions it's a criminal offence.

If you live and work in the U.S. you can hire a lawyer on a contingency basis (*i.e.* he or she only gets paid if a settlement is made in your favor). And oddly enough, the deeper the pockets of the perpetrator, the more worthwhile it is to file a lawsuit.

Among other things, you will have to prove that you are the author of the original work, that the perpetrator had access to your work, and that your work originated before the plagiarized version.

That's why writers register their screenplays and teleplays, as well as treatments, with a Copyright Office and the WGA, so they can prove who wrote the piece and when. (See the section Registering your work.)

The TV business—how not to die like a dog

"The TV business is uglier than most things. It is normally perceived as some kind of cruel and shallow money trench through the heart of the journalism industry, a long plastic hallway where thieves and pimps run free and good men die like dogs, for no good reason."
http://tinyurl.com/ThompsonHS
    —Hunter S. Thompson, *Generation of Swine*

Most scriptwriters write for television. There is no Option and Purchase agreement in their world unless they write a spec feature and sell it.

Scriptwriters are doomed to share their credit with someone else. They don't customarily possess the copyright to their work, but they *do* (if lucky) usually end up possessing a credit for each successive show or episode they write.

In the television world, credits generate residuals—big or small payments that come in mighty handy if a writer is out of work for a spell.

Here is the tale of Alice, not in Wonderland, but in the "cruel and shallow money trench..." that is the television business.

"Alice" is a writer I correspond with, and here is her story. A very substantial production company with a boatload of credits and deep pockets contracts Alice to write a pilot for a television series based on an idea supplied by the production company. This is a *big* project with high production value, which will almost certainly throw off lucrative profits and residuals.

So, big responsibility for Alice, who works her guts out. The producer works his guts out, too—putting her through numerous rewrites (which exceed local Guild rules). Alice toils on without complaint, hoping to deliver a super piece of work that will do her and her employer proud.

She is not only a skilled, very creative writer. She is a meticulous record keeper. She diligently submits to the Guild copies of all her contracts and dates of delivery of outline and script material.

But that's not all. Because the story-editor who reviews Alice's work has a bad memory, subject to frequent lapses, Alice keeps meticulous records of all communications back and forth. She takes notes during phone calls, keeps copies of all script material, and makes sure the documents bear computer date stamps. The process carries on. Alice delivers the script. The production company says great, thank you very much, all is well.

Some time later, Alice gets a call from her Writer's Guild advising her that the director has rewritten the script and wants to remove the writer's name from the credits. Whoa!!!

Alice objects (naturally) and the dispute goes into arbitration according to Guild procedure. The Director has completely rewritten all the dialogue and changed the plot substantially and makes his claim that Alice should not get a credit because there is nothing left of her work.

According to the guild procedure, dialogue changes do not take first priority in judging entitlement to credits. What does take precedence is a combination of a) significant elements of the plot, b) character creation and c) basic story elements.

At the time of writing, Alice had no inkling that anyone would try to steal her right to a credit, and thus to lucrative residuals (not to mention fame). Had she not coincidentally documented and dated every significant piece of paper, taken notes on phone calls, and dated both of these, *she could still have lost the arbitration.*

Writer beware.

Alice had kept all her records in two banker boxes, almost full. By submitting these documents, she proved the particulars of her authorship, and verified all events that took place from the date of the first pitch meeting through to delivery of the final draft. The arbitration panel, impressed by Alice's diligence, and unimpressed by certain instances of prevarication by the director, ruled in favor of Alice, and her credit was retained.

Here's the kicker of this tale. Since the end of the arbitration, Alice has added to her coffers over $10,000 in residual payments. The good news for all writers is that it *is* possible to prevent predators from stealing your story.

Questions and answers

Q. I was told not too long ago that a quick way to establish a copyright is to put a "C" at the top of one's synopsis with a circle around the "C," put the synopsis in an envelope, and mail it to one's self. Do not ever open the envelope unless a need arises to prove the copyright.

Is this a legitimate method and is it legally binding?

BARRY: What you're saying is true up to a point. What you describe is the "do-it-yourself" protection, except that you must send it by REGISTERED mail. This only proves that the material in the envelope existed at a particular point in time. It is not necessarily proof that you wrote it. It can be a good piece of evidence if you have to go to court, but it's much stronger to have lodged copyright with the Library of Congress.

Also, it's absolutely necessary to register your script, outline, or treatment with WGA if you're going to send it out to markets in the U.S. The reason for this is that an accepted assumption has grown up in parts of the industry that material registered with the WGA is more likely to be legitimate and not plagiarized. It would be a good idea to put the WGA registration number on the bottom left of your cover page below your name and contact information.

Q. I participated in an online "class" tonight with Ed Solomon (*Men in Black*). My question concerned whether he saw a downside to submitting a brief (500 word max) treatment if I had a more detailed treatment registered. He said there was practically zero chance of a studio/producer stealing the idea, as the legal fees would quickly exceed what it would take to option it. He did indicate there was some concern that "losers" would "attach" themselves to it. Does he mean that other writers might claim it was their idea?

BARRY: I can't be sure what Ed meant by that remark. Possibly your interpretation is correct. Or perhaps he was alluding to the possibility that a "Loser Producer" would hire his own writer to create a screenplay from your idea.

[Note: Once a work is registered with the U.S. Copyright office, there exists proof that it's protected by copyright. But copyright doesn't protect the idea underlying the 500 words. Only the words themselves are safe.]

Q. As a patented (3 time) inventor I would always confer with my patent attorney before I would work extensively on an idea. I feel like I need to consult with an entertainment lawyer before I submit even a simple treatment to EW [Entertainment Weekly]. Do you think I am being too anal?

BARRY: Yes. Literary copyrights are significantly different from patents. I believe that the tests applied to written works are not as onerous as those applied to patents.

Q. Would a simple WGA registration of an outline "generally" be sufficient to protect one's work before I could obtain a complete copyright on the finished script?

BARRY: Your work is copyrighted in manuscript (see Copyright in manuscript section), but you need to understand that literary copyright from the U.S. Copyright Office is fairly easy to obtain online. You also need to understand that (with rare exceptions) you cannot copyright a title, or an idea. That may seem odd or unfair to you, but it is true.

There is no way that I know of to protect your inspiration for the outline, whatever that inspiration might have been. And you cannot copyright a treatment if it is only "in your head."

Q. I am writing a historical drama. The two main characters are fictional, but connected in a unique way to a former U.S. president. I plan on doing all the necessary interviews and research, for it's important to me and the film that this man be accurately portrayed. I will be going this weekend to his presidential library. Currently, I have my outline written, as well as a good logline. My problem is that important elements of the plot are contingent upon rather obscure historical references. I can research such things on my own in private. However, I know I will eventually seek the support, as well as the input, of his family and foundation, for I feel the story would greatly benefit [from the interviews]. I realize historical events are in the public domain, but it's the unique twist on such events about which I am writing.

To what extent, and in what fashion can I discuss the film with the family and media relations, and still feel my story is protected?

Also, could you suggest anyone that might speak with me on this matter?

BARRY: Ideas are not copyrightable, so other people can use your ideas if they choose, but they cannot use your embodiment of the idea. Therefore, since you have written an outline and created two fictional characters, it is imperative that you at least get these ideas submitted on paper (or computer file) to the Library of Congress Copyright Office. You should also register your work with the WGA.

You can never have a guarantee that someone won't take your basic idea and write their own story about it, so your detailed material, and registration of your own written records might become valuable as the substance of a lawsuit if that ever happens.

Please be meticulous about dating everything you write, and diarizing telephone conversations in your research.

I recommend that you speak to your lawyer about how to protect yourself, and he or she might advise you about what steps you need to take, or else pass you on to a copyright specialist.

Q. A few weeks ago I finished my first script. For the moment I'm working with the second draft.

The script is an adaptation and I haven't got the rights. What do I do to get 'em?

BARRY: If it's a novel you are adapting, you write a query to the publisher asking if the rights have already been optioned, and if not, ask who you need to speak to about acquiring the rights.

Then you need to come up with some money to pay for the option (whatever you negotiate), and to hire a lawyer to draft an Option and Purchase Agreement.

Q2. Should I speak to the author?

BARRY: Not unless the author controls the rights.

Q3. Is it okay for me to show the script to a producer, screenwriter or a director without having to buy the rights?

BARRY: Yes, but you need to ascertain whether or not the rights are available, and to protect yourself, you need to state in writing to the recipient of your screenplay, that, although the rights are available, you have NOT acquired them.

This is a risky procedure, because the producer, screenwriter, or director could go and option the rights and write the script or have it written, cutting you entirely out of the picture. My advice: don't do it.

On the other hand, if the rights are NOT available, you could send your script out stipulating in writing in your query and submission letter that this is a sample of your work and skill at adaptation, but telling the recipient that the rights to the original work have already been optioned. In this latter case, you will have written a "spec sample script" that is not saleable, until or unless the current rights holder wants to buy it. The odds of that happening are about the same as the odds of winning the National Lottery of Ireland (currently approximately 1 in 8,145,060).

Q. I'm in the process of finishing writing a comedy screenplay that I feel is going to be the biggest thing since the Simpsons (only it's not a cartoon). This is the funniest thing ever. And it has never been done before, so I'm very positive that it will be a hit. I currently work in Advertising, and the creative director in my agency was a writer for Mork and Mindy and various other projects so I was hoping to present it to him when I'm done.

BARRY: First, some unsolicited advice. It's wonderful that you have so much pride in your work, and that you have all that confidence. You'll need it if you become a screenwriter. Screenwriting is not for sissies, but even though you feel your screenplay is the best thing to come along since the computer chip, don't—please don't—tell anybody else how great it is. You're inviting contempt right out of the gate.

Q2. However, I want some advice on what happens when you already sell the script, do you lose all rights, or is it still yours?

BARRY: When you sell your car, is it still yours? Obviously not. Same with a screenplay. Except that a good writer's contract will usually leave you with rights to royalties, and sometimes a profit share. Depends on your bargaining strength.

Q3. Also writing a screenplay, is it as lucrative as it seems? Or should you not give up your day job. I know I sound overconfident, but everyone who reads some of this claims it's the funniest thing ever.

BARRY: Screenwriting can be very lucrative—but don't give up your day job until you have so many offers to pay for your services that you don't have the time to accept them.

Any producer who gets your script made into a movie will also typically acquire the ancillary and remake rights. But you should not sign any deal that is an outright sale. You should be getting a preset fee for remake or sequel or television rights.

Q4. So I'm sure it will be a hit, I just know the possibilities of the character I created, and I know it can be marketed like Star Wars. So how can I own the rights to these characters. I'm thankful for whatever advice you can give me.

BARRY: If you should be lucky enough to get an offer for your screenplay, you need to get an agent and an entertainment lawyer, which is easy to do when you have a *bona fide* offer, hard to do when you don't. They will negotiate ownership of the rights, and residual payments.

Q. I have a question that no one I have asked seems to be able to answer. I am very new to script writing and I am thinking about writing a script based on the life of an athlete from the early 1900's. My concern is with legality. I was wondering if you could tell me what is necessary for me to do. This athlete died in the 1940's so I am not fully sure to whom his estate belongs. Also, if he does not have an established estate, am I free to write? Some people told me I have to obtain legal rights while others said I can just write. Also, several books have been written about him, and many of the things I plan to include in the script, if I write it, will be stuff covered in the books. I was wondering if there is a legality issue there too. Since the books are biographies, it is inevitable that I would use similar information.

BARRY: This is a very well detailed question. I've had fairly extensive experience in this area, but I caution you that I am not a lawyer and do not give or purport to give legal advice. I strongly recommend that before you write, you seek legal counsel. It's well worth the few bucks.

In general the following has been my experience: one is free to write about someone who was a public figure, who is now deceased, without obtaining any legal rights from his heirs or assigns. You may, however, wish to secure the co-operation of any family members who may have information that would be useful to you.

If you do a taped interview with someone, and you tell them you are going to write a screenplay about the sports figure you are going to portray, you are usually free to use information thus gained, provided you don't egregiously twist the information given. To be perfectly safe, you should have a lawyer provide you with a release form that you could get the interviewee to sign. The interviewee would typically get a "Thanks to" credit in the tail credits of the film.

Newspaper reports are in the public domain, but the work of columnists, like Dan Savage, Dave Barry, Noam Chomsky, or the late Molly Ivins, is copyright and may not be used without their permission.

Publications published prior to January 1, 1923 are in the public domain and may be used freely.

You may use the information in a copyrighted work for research, but you will be infringing copyright if you copy the author's expression of the information and present it as your own work.

In other words, you cannot pass off the exact, or nearly exact, words used by another author to express an idea unless you credit that author.

If your athlete or anyone else published a book on his athletic career and you wanted to use it, you would be well advised to acquire the rights to it. To do that, you require the services of a lawyer.

Q. Suppose I write a screenplay on Hitler or George Patton and the only sources available are books and documentaries available on something like National Geographic or PBS specials. Would I need to option any of these works beforehand?

I won't use any of the words directly from the material because my writing is more of a reinvention like "The Pianist."

But then how would I have gotten the information without their blueprint, right?

BARRY: I'll first give you my standard caveat: I strongly recommend that before you write an adaptation or a screenplay based on other works, you seek legal counsel.

It is my understanding that if someone sues you for copyright infringement, one of the things they need to prove is that you had access to (or likely had access to) the allegedly infringed work. But I have been told that they would also need to prove that you used the embodiment of their ideas. The way I understand this is, for example, if the PBS Special narrative said, "George Patton epitomized the spirit of the frontier gunslinger," and if one of the characters in your screenplay says, "George Patton epitomizes the spirit of the gunslinger," that sentence is close enough to their original embodiment of the idea that you could be deemed to be infringing their copyright.

If, on the other hand, your character said, "Patton carries a silver .45 on his hip like a gunslinger," you could have derived that sentence from any number of sources, and the only word in common is gunslinger, which is probably not distinctive enough to claim infringement. But if you had 50 such similarities to an original work, you still might have a problem.

When one relies on source works for facts or information, especially if those facts are available from several sources, you would likely be safe to use them, but you must be careful to present such ideas in your own words.

Since screenplays consist mainly of speeches and descriptions of events and actions, infringement is less likely if your subject matter is historical and is a popular topic about which much has been reported in the past.

In my book *The Boyd Gang*, which I co-wrote with Marjorie Lamb, and in my subsequent movie *The Life and Times of Edwin Alonzo Boyd*, we relied on quotes that were published in newspapers. (Quotes from newspaper news reports are in the public domain.) My second source was a taped interview that we did with Edwin Alonzo Boyd—a notorious bank robber in Toronto in the 1950s, who at the time of our interview was on lifetime parole. Under a signed contract, we paid him a small expenses fee for the interview and got a signed release to use the recorded material.

My recommendation would be that if you're writing about a very public figure, go to your public library or archive and pillage newspapers for actual quotes that you can use as dialogue and then invent the rest. In the case of your PBS special, I'd be surprised if most of their material did not come from newspaper and other public domain documentary accounts.

If the books that are your references cite their sources as newspapers, it seems you would be free to use such quoted material even though you didn't get it from the original newspaper, because it is public domain material.

Q2. Also, for fiction works, do you need to own the rights to adapt it? Are Shakespeare and Jane Austen the exceptions?

BARRY: Published works fall into the public domain after a certain period of time, or in special cases, where the original authors failed to renew their copyright.

The University of North Carolina has an excellent table "When U.S. Works Pass into the Public Domain" **http://tinyurl.com/PublicDomainWhen** that lays out the dates and length of protection of published works in the U.S.

Certain public domain works spawn tangled and contradictory opinions and require a legal specialist to sort out. Here's an example – an exchange between me and one of my correspondents on the AllExperts site:
http://tinyurl.com/ExpertBarry

Q. How can I find out who owns the rights to Sherlock Holmes and how to get permission to write a story? I emailed the Estate.

BARRY: Herein lies a tangled tale. Sherlockian.net at

http://tinyurl.com/SherlockRights offers a synopsis of the rights, which contains the following information.

Copyright in the Sherlock Holmes stories expired in Canada in 1980. Copyright on Arthur Conan Doyle's work in the United Kingdom expired at the end of the year 2000.

In the United States, the only Sherlock Holmes publications remaining in copyright are ten short stories in a twelve-story collection originally named *The Case-Book of Sherlock Holmes*.

Two stories in the collection, "The Adventure of the Mazarin Stone" and "The Problem of Thor Bridge" (published 1921 and 1922) are in the public domain in the U.S. and the rest of the world.
The remaining ten stories http://tinyurl.com/HolmesTenStories
are the only Sherlock Holmes works still under copyright in the U.S., and they will begin to fall into the public domain there in 2019.

A further twist concerns the characters of the Sherlock Holmes stories. (In 2009 when J.D. Salinger sued John Colting to block the publication of Colting's book, which appropriated the character of Holden Caulfied, an injunction was granted, but later vacated, leaving Colting's lawyers free to proceed to trial. The parties settled among themselves, but this precedent seems to indicate that any party attempting to prevent authors from using the Doyle characters would not get a welcome inside the courthouse).

In fact a suit has been lodged to clear the way for writers to use Sherlock and Watson. On February 14th, 2013, the following report was posted on a website named *Free Sherlock:*

A civil action was filed today in the United States District Court for the Northern District of Illinois against the Arthur Conan Doyle Estate by Sherlock Holmes scholar Leslie S. Klinger. Klinger seeks to have the Court determine that the characters of Sherlock Holmes and Dr. John H. Watson are no longer protected by federal copyright laws and that writers, filmmakers, and others are free to create new stories about Holmes, Watson, and others of their circle without paying license fees to the current owners of the remaining copyrights.

Klinger says that the litigation came about because he and Laurie R. King, best-selling author of the "Mary Russell" series of mysteries that also feature Sherlock Holmes, were co-editing a new book called "In the Company of Sherlock Holmes. "This collection of stories by major mystery/sci-fi/fantasy authors inspired by the Holmes tales, is to be published by Pegasus Books. "The Conan Doyle Estate contacted our publisher, " says Klinger, "and implied that if the Estate wasn't paid a license fee, they'd convince the major distributors not to sell the book. Our publisher was, understandably, concerned, and told us that the book couldn't come out unless this was resolved.

"It is true that some of Conan Doyle's stories about Holmes are still protected by the U.S. copyright laws. However, the vast majority of the stories that Conan Doyle wrote are not. The characters of Holmes, Watson, and others are fully established in those fifty 'public-domain' stories. Under U.S. law, this should mean that anyone is free to create new stories about Holmes and Watson.

"This isn't the first time the Estate has put pressure on creators," Klinger adds. "It is the first time anyone has stood up to them. In the past, many simply couldn't afford to fight or to wait for approval, and have given in and paid off the Estate for 'permission.' I'm asking the Court to put a permanent stop to this kind of bullying. Holmes and Watson belong to the world, not to some distant relatives of Arthur Conan Doyle." More at....
http://free-sherlock.com/

Q2. Follow up: Did the filmmakers of the Robert Downey Jr. movie have to pay for rights? Thought I read that somewhere.

BARRY: I don't have access to the filmmakers' legal agreements, but my understanding is that they couldn't have been forced to make rights payments for the original Conan Doyle works unless they needed the rights from the eleven stories still under copyright in the U.S.

However, many people have written new works using the characters (which they have the right to do because those characters are also in the public domain). Such new works can be copyrighted. If a filmmaker wanted to use material in such new works, he or she would have to deal with the copyright owner.

You can see an example of such work here.
http://tinyurl.com/NewAuthorOfHolmes

If the producers and writers of the movie based their movie on a later work written by someone other than Conan Doyle, they might have paid for those rights. In your case, if you wish to use the Sherlock Holmes stories, you need to make sure you're using the public domain versions.

Q3. Follow up: When I asked who owns the rights to Sherlock Holmes, you wrote [that] it's not necessary to deal with the Estate. A link in your reply took me to a site which stated:

"The American copyrights are owned by Conan Doyle Estate Ltd. The American agent for administering them, and related rights in the Sherlock Holmes character, is Jon Lellenberg." Can you explain this? Some say you can write a Holmes story as long as it is different and not taken directly from the original.

BARRY: Lellenberg may be the administrator of the ten stories still in the public domain. If a writer appropriated any "written expression" from those ten stories, he or she would be infringing copyright. But a writer may use any or all parts of a public domain work.

Summary of how
to protect your work

Here's a recap of important things you need to understand and do to protect your literary works so that others don't steal your story, or the benefits of your story.

1. Your story is "copyright in manuscript." Therefore, everything you put down on paper is your literary property and no one can make use of it legally except you. You are the sole person who can grant others the right to use your literary property.

2. You can (and should) register your copyright with the U.S. Copyright Office and/or the appropriate Copyright Office of your country.

3. Facts are not copyrightable. Therefore, you may use facts that you find in the work of others, and reciprocally, others may use facts they find in your work.

4. If you use facts that you find in other writers' works, be scrupulous in describing those facts in words and phrases that are original to you.

5. In your own work you are free to use verbatim anything that is in the Public Domain, but be aware that your copyright only protects the parts of your work that are original to you.

6. Other writers, depending on the circumstances, may legally use parts of your copyrighted work if they give you appropriate credit, and if they get your permission to do so.

7. Some writers, especially reviewers, or film critics, for example, may quote from your works relying on the "Fair Use" exception, without getting your permission.

8. Do not proceed to work under an "implied-in-fact" contract like Eric Ryder, who is currently suing the director and producers of

Avatar. Don't be shy or afraid of asking for a memorandum of intent, or a deal memo, or something in writing that crystallizes the intentions of both parties. Above all, consult a lawyer. The money spent is worth it.

9. In your own writing, if you use other authors' work as research, avoid utilizing plot points without expressing them in your own way so that you don't provide fodder for litigation after your work is published or made into a movie.

10. Resist the temptation to talk about the details of a project or story idea you are working on. Oral expression by itself is not copyrightable. Others may use those ideas legally in a written work.

11. In the "query" stage, or the pitch stage, or the "screenplay circulation stage," keep a detailed record of whom you have approached. Lay a "paper trail" with your e-mails and collect them in a segregated file.

12. If you designate another person (be it agent, friend, finder, producer, etc.) to "shop" your script by pitching your project to someone he or she knows, put the conditions of such pitching in writing. Best approach is to consult a lawyer as to what should be written. Avoid giving these kinds of permissions orally. It could turn out to be a mess, or pre-empt your own pitching. Tread carefully.

13. When you get an offer, that's the time to consult your agent, if you have one, or your lawyer, as to what steps should be taken to respond to the offer, so that your story can't be (metaphorically) stolen by the buyer.

14. Learn how the Option and Purchase procedure operates, so you can make good judgments, and direct your agent or lawyer intelligently.

15. As you write your story, build your "Chain of Title" by keeping a diary of how your writing began and how it got

developed. Sometimes you may attract development funds or other assistance. Keep a record of events. Keep dated copies of the various versions of your writing. Be ready for the moment (which we hope never happens) when you are called upon to prove when, where, and how you come into possession of your story.

16. You may decide at some point to write a story in collaboration with another writer. Talk all you want with the proposed co-writer. But do not commit a word to paper concerning the story until both you and your proposed writing partner have agreed upon a written contract or deal memo that you will both show to your lawyers for input or amendment. Do not put yourself in a position that leaves you with a screenplay that you cannot circulate because there is a "cloud on title." And especially do not allow yourself to be put in a position where your literary property is worthless.

My web site: **http://tinyurl.com/barryswebsite**

E-mail Barry at barry@barrypearson.com

Sample of an
Option and Purchase Agreement

Please note that this is a sample only. Consult your lawyer for a suitable agreement for your situation.

OPTION AGREEMENT

-AND-

PURCHASE AGREEMENT

Between

PRODUCER

(Address)

"Purchaser"

- and –

WRITER

(Address)

OPTION AGREEMENT

THIS AGREEMENT made as of the __day of _____, (year)

BETWEEN:

PRODUCER

(Address)

(hereinafter referred to as "Purchaser")

- and -

WRITER

(Address)

(hereinafter referred to as "The Writer")

WITNESSETH THAT:

WHEREAS the Writer has the sole and exclusive right throughout the world to grant all of the rights granted hereunder in and to the literary work entitled "[Name of Work]" (which literary work together with the themes, plot, structure, research, title, dialogue, descriptions, translations, sequences and all versions including all copyrights therein are herein together referred to as the "Property"), written by (Name of Writer) (hereinafter referred to as "Writer");

AND WHEREAS Purchaser intends, but does not undertake, to produce or cause to be produced a motion picture or motion pictures and/or television productions based upon, suggested by or adapted from the Property;

AND WHEREAS the Purchaser, beginning immediately upon signing, undertakes to cause to be written, a Screenplay from the Property, and intends to use said Screenplay in the raising of funding to make a production from the Property;

AND WHEREAS Purchaser, relying upon the representation and warranties of the Writer set forth herein, desires to acquire from the Writer the rights hereinafter described upon the terms and conditions hereinafter set forth.

NOW THEREFORE in consideration of the mutual covenants and agreements set forth in this Agreement and for the sum of $10.00 and other good and valuable consideration (the receipt and sufficiency of which is acknowledged by the parties), the parties agree as follows:

1. OPTION

Grant of Option - Writer hereby grants to Purchaser an exclusive and irrevocable option (hereinafter referred to as the "Option") for six (6) months (hereinafter referred to as the "Initial Option Period"), commencing as of the date hereof, to acquire the television, motion picture and all ancillary rights (as more specifically set forth in Section 1 of the Purchase Agreement between the parties, annexed hereto as Schedule "A" and hereinafter referred to as the "Purchase Agreement") in and to the Property

First Option Extension Period - If Purchaser does not exercise the Option during the Initial Option Period, the Writer hereby grants to Purchaser the option (exercisable in the sole discretion of Purchaser) to extend the Option for a grace period of ten (10) days (the "Option Extension Period") commencing on the first day following the expiration date of the Initial Option Period. Purchaser shall notify the Writer of any such extension of the Option in writing no later than one (1) day before the expiration date of the Initial Option Period

Contingent Option Extension Period - If within the first six months of the Option period, Purchaser makes application to a development fund granting body, such as (Name of Funding Body), or any other granting institution, which requires a specific Option period longer than the Option then existing, the Writer agrees that the Initial Option Period shall be automatically extended from the date of receipt of funds from such body to a date which conforms with the requirement of the fund granting body, but which is not more than twenty-four (24) months from said date. The Purchaser shall notify Writer in writing of such automatic extension not later than 30 days from receipt of abovementioned funds

Preproduction Option Extension Period – During the Initial Option Period, the First Option Extension Period, or the Contingent Option Extension Period, Purchaser may, at its sole discretion, upon payment of $2000 extend the option period for six (6)

months. If before or upon the last day of the Preproduction Extension Period, the first day of principal production has not occurred, the Option Agreement and the Purchase Agreement shall be deemed null and void, and all rights shall revert to the Writer. Writer shall retain the $2000 and shall have no further obligation to the Purchaser, and the Purchaser shall have no further obligation to the Writer.

2. FEE FOR OPTION

2.01 Initial Option Period - Purchaser agrees to notify the Writer of receipt of any and all development funds within fifteen (15) days of such receipt, and to pay, from such development funds, the Writer a sum of $____.

3. EXERCISE OF OPTION

3.01 Exercise - The Option may be exercised by notice in writing served upon the Writer by or on behalf of Purchaser at any time within the option periods hereinabove specified. If principal photography of any production based on the Property is commenced by or on behalf of the Purchaser prior to written notice of the exercise of the Option, the Option shall be deemed to have been exercised on the date of the commencement of such principal photography. Upon the exercise of the Option, the purchase price specified in Section 3 of the Purchase Agreement shall become payable in accordance with the terms of the Purchase Agreement.

3.02 Expiration of Option - Subject to Section 3.03 (Third Party Claims) and/or Section 4.02 (Force Majeure) hereof, if Purchaser fails to exercise the Option during the Initial Option Period, or the First Option Extension Period (as applicable), or the Contingent Option Extension Period (as applicable), or the Preproduction Option Extension Period (as applicable), the Option shall lapse, the Purchase Agreement shall be null and void and any amounts paid to the Writer hereunder shall be and remain the sole property of the Writer.

3.03 Effect of Third Party Claim on Option Period - Without limiting any other rights Purchaser may have, the Writer hereby agrees that if there is any third party claim and/or litigation involving any breach or alleged breach of any of the representations and warranties of the Writer contained or incorporated herein, the Initial Option Period, the First Option Extension Period or the Second Option Extension Period (whichever is then current) shall automatically be extended until no claim and/or litigation involving any breach or alleged breach of any such representations or warranties of the Writer is outstanding. If at any time after the occurrence of such claim and/or litigation, such claim and/or litigation is not resolved to the reasonable satisfaction of Purchaser, Purchaser may, in addition to any other rights and remedies Purchaser may have, rescind this Agreement and in such event notwithstanding any contrary provisions elsewhere in this Agreement, the Writer hereby agrees to repay Purchaser any amounts paid by Purchaser hereunder in connection with the Property.

4. RIGHTS DURING OPTION PERIOD

4.01 Permitted Activities -the Writer acknowledges that Purchaser may, during the initial Option Period, the First Option Extension Period, the Contingent Option Extension Period, or the Preproduction Option Extension Period, whether or not Purchaser has exercised or will thereafter exercise the Option, undertake production and pre-production activities in connection with any of the rights optioned hereunder including, without limiting the generality of the foregoing, negotiating and/or entering into financing or distribution agreements relating to motion picture or television production based on the Property, and/or the preparation and submission of treatments, stories, screen stories, teleplays and/or screenplays based on the Property.

4.02 Force Majeure - If the engagement in any preproduction activities in connection with any version of the Property to be produced hereunder, including the writing of any treatments, stories, screen stories, teleplays and/or screenplays based on the Property, shall be prevented or interrupted due to epidemic, fire, action of the elements, strikes, labor disputes, governmental order, court order, act of God, public enemy, wars, riots, or civil commotion, the Initial Option Period, the First Option Extension Period and/or the Contingent Option Extension Period, as applicable, shall be extended for the number of days such event of force majeure exists.

5. PURCHASE AGREEMENT

5.01 Entry Into Purchase Agreement - Effective upon the exercise of the Option by the Purchaser pursuant to the provisions of this Agreement, Purchaser and Writer shall enter into the Purchase Agreement. Purchaser shall notify Writer in writing upon the exercise of the Option by Purchaser that Option has been exercised.

5.02 Prior Execution of Purchase Agreement - Concurrently with the execution of this Agreement, the Writer and Purchaser have executed the Purchase Agreement which is undated, it being agreed that effective upon the exercise of the Option by Purchaser in accordance with this Agreement (but not otherwise) the signatures of Writer and Purchaser to the Purchase Agreement shall be deemed to be effective and the Purchase Agreement shall constitute a valid and binding agreement and assignment effective as of the date of exercise of the Option and Purchaser is hereby authorized and empowered to date the Purchase Agreement accordingly.

5.03 Additional Execution of Copies of Purchase Agreement - If Purchaser exercises the Option, Purchaser shall deliver to the Writer copies of the Purchase Agreement, dated as of the date of the exercise of the Option, and the Writer shall, if so requested by Purchaser, execute and deliver to the Purchaser additional copies of the Purchase Agreement.

5.04 Deemed Vesting of Rights in Purchaser - Notwithstanding the failure or omission of either party hereto to execute and/or deliver such additional documents as mentioned herein, it is agreed that, upon the exercise of the Option by Purchaser in accordance with this Agreement, all rights agreed to be transferred to Purchaser pursuant to the provisions of the Purchase Agreement shall be deemed to be vested in Purchaser, effective as of the date of the exercise of the Option.

5.05 Void Purchase Agreement - If Purchaser fails to exercise the Option in accordance with this Agreement upon the expiration of the Option, the signatures of the Writer and Purchaser to the Purchase Agreement shall be null and void and of no further force or effect whatsoever, and Purchaser shall be deemed not to have acquired any Rights other than the Option.

6. REPRESENTATIONS AND WARRANTIES

6.01 Incorporation of Representations and Warranties - All of the representations and warranties of the Writer contained in the Purchase Agreement and any and all provisions thereof requiring the Writer to maintain and protect the copyrights in and to the Property shall be deemed incorporated herein by reference with the same force and effect as though set out herein in full and shall be applicable through the Initial Option Period, the First Option Extension Period and/or the Second Option Extension Period (as applicable), and/or the Preproduction Option Extension Period, and shall survive any exercise of the Option or expiration thereof without time limit.

7. NEGATIVE COVENANT Of Writer

7.01 Negative Covenant - the Writer agrees that Writer shall not, at any time during the Initial Option Period, the First Option Extension Period or the Contingent Option Extension Period (as applicable), and/or the Preproduction Option Extension Period, exercise or authorize or permit the exercise of others of any of the rights covered by this Agreement.

8. ADDITIONAL DOCUMENTS

8.01 Further Documents - the Writer agrees to execute, acknowledge and deliver to Purchaser and/or procure the execution, acknowledgement and deliver to Purchaser of any additional documents or instruments which Purchaser may reasonably require to fully effectuate and carry out the intent and purposes of this Agreement and/or to convey to Purchaser good and marketable title in and to the Property in the event the Option is exercised by Purchaser, including without limitation an Acknowledgement, Release and Indemnity from the Writer in the form attached to the Purchase Agreement as Schedule "B". Without limiting the generality of the foregoing, if directed by Purchaser (or its counsel), the Writer agrees to execute and deliver to Purchaser a short form option agreement or short form assignment agreement, each in form satisfactory to Purchaser, which instruments may be recorded by the Purchaser with the United States and/or any foreign Copyright Office(s) as evidence of the Option, or upon exercise of the Option, the Rights to the Property herein granted to the Purchaser.

8.02 Attorney-In-Fact – If the Writer fails to execute, acknowledge or deliver to Purchaser any agreements, assignments or other instruments to be executed, acknowledged and/or delivered by the Writer hereunder (including as reasonably required by Purchaser pursuant to Section 8.01 hereof), then Purchaser is hereby appointed the Writer's attorney-in-fact with full right, power, and authority to execute, acknowledge and deliver the same in the name of and on behalf of the Writer.

9. ASSIGNMENT AND SURVIVABILITY

9.01 Permitted Assigns - This Agreement may not be assigned by the Writer without the prior written consent of Purchaser. Purchaser may not assign this Agreement without the prior written consent of the Writer. Any assignee of either the Writer or Purchaser must agree to be bound by the provisions of this Agreement. This Agreement shall enure to the benefit of the Writer's successors and any assigns permitted by Purchaser and to the benefit of Purchaser's successors, licensees, and assigns.

10. NOTICES AND PAYMENTS

10.01 Providing Notice - Any notice required or permitted to be given hereunder shall be in writing and any such notice, or any payment to be made hereunder shall be delivered in person or via courier or mailed by pre-paid registered post, and shall be deemed to have been received by the party to whom it is directed when delivered or, if by pre-paid registered mail, five (5) days after the mailing thereof, any such notice shall be addressed to the parties at their addresses respectively set forth on the first page of this Agreement, provided that either party may change the notification address of such party by notice given as aforesaid; all payments hereunder shall be delivered as aforesaid by check made payable as instructed in writing by the Writer.

11. MISCELLANEOUS

11.01 Section Headings - The headings of paragraphs, sections and other subdivisions of this Agreement are for convenience of reference only and shall not be used in any way to govern, limit, modify or construe this Agreement or any part or provision thereof or otherwise be given any legal effect.

11.02 Conflicting Laws, etc. - If for any reason any provision(s) of this Agreement shall conflict with any statute, law, regulation or ordinance to be found to be void, voidable or unenforceable for any reason, then such provision(s) shall be deemed severed from the remainder of this Agreement, but in such event the provision of this Agreement shall be severed or modified only to the extent necessary to conform with such requirements, and the remainder of this Agreement shall continue in full force and effect.

11.03 No Waiver - No Waiver by either party of any breach by either party of any covenant or condition of this Agreement shall be deemed a waiver of any other breach (whether prior to or subsequent) of the same or any other covenant or condition of this Agreement or any other agreement.

11.04 Entire Agreement - This Agreement and the terms and conditions hereof express the entire understanding and agreement of the parties hereto and replace any and all prior agreements or understandings, whether written or oral, relating to the subject matter of this agreement.

11.05 Amendment - This Agreement cannot be modified or amended except by written instrument signed by the parties hereto.

11.06 No Partnership - Nothing herein contained shall be construed to create a partnership or joint venture by or between the parties or to make either of the parties the agent of the other.

11.07 Governing Law - This Agreement shall be governed by the laws of (Name of Jurisdiction) applicable therein.

11.08 Copies of the Property and underlying materials – upon signing of this agreement the Writer agrees to provide Purchaser with one copy of the Property and of all resource and reference material in their possession and Purchaser shall reimburse Writer for the copying costs of such materials.

11.09 Consultation – Writer agrees to make himself available to consult periodically, at his convenience, and on a reasonable basis, with the Purchaser and/or its designees, with regard to matters of story research and story authenticity in areas wherein he may have knowledge and information.

IN WITNESS WHEREOF the parties have executed this Agreement as of the date first written above.

PRODUCER

Per: _____

WRITER _____

SCHEDULE "A"

PURCHASE AGREEMENT

THIS AGREEMENT made as of the _____ day of _____, _____.

BETWEEN:

PRODUCER

(Address)

(hereinafter referred to as "Purchaser")

- and -

WRITER

(Address)

(hereinafter referred to as "The Writer")

WITNESSETH THAT:

WHEREAS the Writer has the sole and exclusive right throughout the world to grant all of the rights granted hereunder in and to the literary work described as follows:

Title: (Title of Work)

Written by: (Name of Writer), (hereinafter referred to as "Writer")

(which literary work together with the themes, plot, structure, research, title, dialogue, descriptions, translations, sequences and all versions including all copyrights therein are herein together referred to as the "Property");

AND WHEREAS Purchaser intends but does not undertake, to produce or cause to be produced a motion picture or television production based upon, suggested by, or adapted from the Property;

AND WHEREAS Purchaser, relying upon the Writer's representations and warranties herein, desires to acquire the rights hereinafter described upon the terms and conditions hereinafter set forth;

NOW THEREFORE in consideration of the mutual covenants and agreements set forth in this Agreement and for other good and valuable consideration (the receipt and sufficiency of which is acknowledged by the parties), the parties agree as follows:

1. GRANT OF RIGHTS

The Writer hereby sells, grants, conveys and assigns exclusively to Purchaser all television (including series), theatrical, silent, sound, and musical film and motion picture ("Motion Pictures") rights, together with all ancillary rights specified below in and to the Property, throughout the world, without time limit. The rights granted to Purchaser hereunder (without limiting the grant of rights hereinabove made) include the following sole and exclusive rights throughout the world in and to the Property:

(a) The right to make, produce, adapt and copyright a motion picture and/or a series of motion pictures fixed in film, tape, disc (compact, computer, laser or otherwise), wire, audiovisual cartridge, cassette or by any other technical process (collectively "Formats") now known or hereafter devised, in any and all sizes, gauges, colors and types, and for such purpose to record and reproduce in synchronization with such motion pictures, spoken words, taken from or based upon the Property, any and all kinds of music, musical accompaniments and/or lyrics to be performed or sung by the performers in any such motion pictures, and any and all other kinds of sound or sound effects;

(b) The right to produce foreign-language versions of any and all Motion Pictures;

(c) The right to exhibit, release, distribute, rent, lease and generally exploit, deal in and with any and all Motion Pictures in any and all Formats in any place whatsoever, including homes, theatres and elsewhere, whether or not a fee is charged directly or indirectly for viewing the Motion Pictures and in any and all media whether now known or hereinafter devised including without limitation television, motion pictures and computer display. For greater certainty, it is acknowledged and agreed that the foregoing includes, without limitation, standard and non-standard television release, theatrical release, non-theatrical release, video-cassette release, CD-ROM, DVD, CD-i and other interactive media release.

(d) For the purpose of advertising, publicizing or exploiting any and all Motion Pictures, the right to broadcast and/or transmit by means of television, radio or any process analogous thereto now known or hereafter devised, all or any part of any and all Motion Pictures and announcements of or concerning the pictures, which broadcasts may be accompanied through the use of living actors performing simultaneously with such broadcast or transmission or by any other method or means now known or hereafter devised.

(e) The right to use the title of the work constituting the Property as the title or sub-title of any and all Motion Pictures, or in Purchaser's sole discretion, to select and use any other title or sub-title;

(f) The right to secure copyright registration in any and all Motion Pictures in Purchaser's own name or otherwise, and to renew such copyrights whenever permitted;

(g) The right to prepare and use excerpts, synopses and summaries from any and all Motion Pictures and the Property (not exceeding 2000 words and not for resale in the case of the Property) in prospectuses, programs, posters, lobby displays, press books, newspapers and periodicals, for the purpose of advertising, publicizing and exploiting any and all Motion Pictures.

(h) The exclusive merchandising rights with respect to the images from any and all Motion Pictures; and

(i) The right to publish a soundtrack album based on any and all Motion Pictures.

2. FINANCIAL TERMS

As full and complete consideration for all of the rights herein granted and assigned to Purchaser, Purchaser agrees to pay to the Writer, and the Writer agrees to accept the following amounts, as applicable:

(a) upon production of the first feature length production, on the first day of principal photography, a writer's fee consistent in all respects with the prevailing WGC rates and conditions, at scale, minus script fees already received.

(b) in the event that a television series is produced first, on the first day of principal photography, a writer's fee consistent in all respects with the prevailing WGC rates and conditions, at scale, minus script fees already received.

(c) on the first day of principal photography of any production subsequent to either of (a) or (b), a writer's fee consistent in all respects with the prevailing WGA rates and conditions, at scale, minus script fees already received.

(d) 10% of any and all gross ancillary revenues received by Purchaser in perpetuity, less Purchaser's disbursements necessary to make the sales. For greater clarity, such revenues may include, but are not limited to: CD and video sales, merchandising, licensing of characters, and published works like novelizations.

3. REPRESENTATION AND WARRANTIES OF WRITER

The Writer represents and warrants to Purchaser that:

(a) The Writer is the sole and exclusive owner throughout the world of any and all rights granted to Purchaser hereunder and the Writer has the full right and authority to enter into this Agreement and to grant Purchaser all of the rights herein granted;

(b) No Motion Picture or other version or adaptation of the Property has heretofore been produced, performed or copyrighted anywhere in the world;

(c) The Writer will not assign or license, and heretofore the Writer has not assigned or licensed, to any other person, firm or corporation, or in any manner encumbered any of the rights in and to the Property, or any element(s) thereof, granted to Purchaser herein, including the title of the Property, and there are no rights, licenses and/or grants of any kind relating to the Property in favor of any third party. There are no claims, litigation or other proceedings pending or threatened, which could impair, limit, diminish or infringe upon the rights in the Property herein granted to Purchaser; and

(d) he Property is wholly original with the Writer, and no incident therein or part thereof is taken from, based upon, or adapted from any other literary material, dramatic work, motion picture, television production, or other creative dramatic work. The full use of the Property by Purchaser pursuant to the rights granted herein, or any partial use thereof, will not violate or infringe upon any copyright belonging to any person, firm, or corporation.

The foregoing representations and warranties shall survive the purchase of the rights contemplated by this Agreement without time limit.

4. INDEMNIFICATION

The Writer shall indemnify Purchaser, its subsidiaries and affiliates, and its and their directors, officers, employees, heirs and assigns (the "Indemnified Parties"), against any and all losses, damages, costs and expenses (including reasonable legal fees) which any or all of the Indemnified Parties may suffer or incur by reason of any breach of any of the representations, warranties and/or agreements herein made by the Writer. And Purchaser shall indemnify the Writer same as above.

5. RIGHT TO LITIGATE

The Writer hereby grants to Purchaser the free and unrestricted right, at Purchaser's expense, to institute in the name of and on behalf of the Writer, or the Writer and Purchaser jointly, any and all actions and proceedings, in law or equity, to enjoin or restrain any infringements of the rights herein granted. The Writer hereby assigns and sets over to Purchaser any and all recoveries obtained in any such action, and the Writer hereby agrees not to compromise, settle, or in any manner interfere with such litigation if brought.

6. PROTECTION OF COPYRIGHT

The Writer hereby undertakes to include in any license for production, promotion, or publication of the operatic version of the Property, as referred to in 2., above, in each and every country where such version of the Property or any translation or other adaptation or version of it is to be produced, promoted, or published, a requirement for a copyright notice to be affixed to each copy of any promotion, publication, program or advertisement or material offered for sale; a requirement that the licensee do whatever necessary to preserve such copyright.

7. EDITORIAL MODIFICATION

Purchaser shall have, with written approval of the writer, the sole and final right to make such changes in, additions to and eliminations from the work constituting the Property and to include in any and all Motion Pictures such language, music, characters, incidents and situations as it in its sole discretion may deem advisable.

8. NEGATIVE COVENANT OF WRITER

The Writer shall not do anything, whether by way of license or grant or otherwise, that will impair, interfere with, or infringe upon the rights herein granted. Purchaser hereby expressly reserves all rights in and to any new material created by Purchaser or under Purchaser's direction or authority, or any new additional characters or other material contained in any and all Motion

Pictures or television, or video productions made by Purchaser or its successors, licensees or assigns.

9. NO OBLIGATION TO PRODUCE

Although Purchaser intends to produce a Motion Picture based on the Property, nothing herein contained shall be construed as obligating it to produce any Motion Picture at any time.

10. CREDIT

Purchaser shall state or cause to be stated on all positive prints writer credits as set out according to the terms and conditions of the prevailing WGC agreement at the time of 1st day of Principal Photography, provided that no casual or inadvertent failure of Purchaser to comply with the provisions of this paragraph, nor any failure by third parties to comply with their agreement with the Purchaser with respect to such provisions, shall constitute a breach of this Agreement by Purchaser and the Writer waives any equitable rights or remedies he may have in the event of any such failure, including, without limitation, the right to restrain, enjoin or otherwise inhibit the exploitation of any and all Motion Pictures, the Owner's sole remedy being an action at law for damages. Purchaser shall use its best efforts to cure prospectively any failure, error, or omission following Purchaser's receipt of written notice thereof.

11. ADDITIONAL INSTRUMENTS

The Writer agrees to execute, acknowledge and deliver to Purchaser and/or procure the execution, acknowledgement and delivery to Purchaser of any additional documents or instruments which Purchaser may reasonably require to fully effectuate and carry out the intent and purposes of this Agreement and/or to convey to Purchaser good and marketable title in and to the Property, including without limitation an Acknowledgement, Release and Indemnity from the Writer in the form attached to this Agreement as Schedule "B". Without limiting the generality of the foregoing, if directed by Purchaser (or its counsel), the Writer agrees to execute and deliver to Purchaser a short form assignment agreement, in form satisfactory to the Purchaser, which instrument may be recorded by the Purchaser with the United States and/or any foreign Copyright Office(s) as evidence of the rights to the Property herein granted to the Purchaser.

12. ATTORNEY-IN-FACT

If the Writer fails to execute, acknowledge or deliver to Purchaser any agreements, assignments or other instruments to be executed, acknowledged and/or delivered by the Writer hereunder (including as reasonably required by Purchaser pursuant to Paragraph 11 hereof), then Purchaser is hereby appointed the Writer's attorney-in-fact with full right, power, and authority to execute, acknowledge and deliver the same in the name of and on behalf of the Writer.

13. ASSIGNMENT AND SURVIVABILITY

This Agreement may not be assigned by the Writer without the prior written consent of Purchaser. Purchaser may not assign this Agreement without the prior written consent of the Writer. This Agreement shall enure to the benefit of the Writer's successors and any assigns permitted by Purchaser and to the benefit of Purchaser's successors, licensees, and assigns.

14. NOTICES

Except as otherwise stated herein, any notice required or permitted to be given hereunder shall be in writing and any such notice, or any payment to be made hereunder shall be delivered in person or via courier or mailed by pre-paid registered post, and shall be deemed to have been received by the party to whom it is directed when delivered or, if by pre-paid registered mail, five (5) days after the mailing thereof, any such notice shall be addressed to the parties at their addresses respectively set forth on the first page of this Agreement, provided that either party may change the notification address of such party by notice given as aforesaid.

The headings of paragraphs, sections and other subdivisions of this Agreement are for convenience of reference only and do not form a part hereof and in no manner modify, interpret or construe the agreement between the parties. This Agreement and the terms and conditions hereof express the entire understanding and agreement of the parties hereto and replace any and all prior agreements or understandings, whether written or oral, relating to the subject matter of this agreement.

15. MODIFICATION

This Agreement cannot be modified or amended except by written instrument or instruments executed by each of the parties hereto.

16. NO WAIVER

The waiver by either party of a breach or default by the other shall not be deemed to constitute a waiver of any preceding or subsequent breach or default of the same or any other provision of this Agreement.

17. GOVERNING LAW

This Agreement shall be governed by the laws of (Name of Jurisdiction) applicable therein.

18. CONDITION PRECEDENT

This Agreement is expressly conditional on the exercise of the Purchaser of the Option contained in the Option Agreement within the time period(s) specified therein; failure to so exercise the Option shall render this Agreement null and void ab initio.

IN WITNESS WHEREOF the parties hereto have executed this Agreement as of the day and year first above written.

PRODUCER

Per:_____

WRITER

SCHEDULE "B"

WRITERS

ACKNOWLEDGEMENT, RELEASE AND INDEMNITY

In consideration of the payment of One Dollar ($1.00) and other good and valuable consideration, receipt of which is acknowledged, the undersigned (hereinafter referred to as "Writer") hereby acknowledges and agrees, for the express benefit of (Name of Producer) (hereinafter referred to as "Purchaser") and its representatives, successors, licensees and assigns forever, that (Name of Writer) has granted to Purchaser the exclusive license to grant, sell and otherwise deal with the worldwide motion picture, video and television rights and all related distribution, exhibition and exploitation rights, including, without limitation, via CD-ROM, DVD, and other interactive media rights (hereinafter collectively referred to as the "Rights"), in or to that certain literary work written by (Name of Writer) and described as follows:

TITLE: (Name of written work) (hereinafter referred to as the "Property")

WRITTEN BY: (Name of Writer)

DATE OF COPYRIGHT IN MANUSCRIPT:[_____]

COPYRIGHT REGISTRATION:[_____]

COPYRIGHT CLAIMANT'S NAME: (Name of Writer)

Writer consents to the publication in any and all languages, in any and all countries of the world, and in any form or media, of excerpts, synopses and summaries, not exceeding 2,000 words in length each, of the Property and further consents to any motion picture or television version thereof (based in whole or in part thereon) and all distribution, exhibition and exploitation thereof, including, without limitation, via CD-ROM, DVD, and other interactive media.

Writer represents and warrants to (Name of Producer) that:

(a) (Name of Writer) is the sole and exclusive author of the Property and is the sole and exclusive licensee throughout the world of any and all rights granted to Purchaser hereunder and that he has the full right and authority to grant (Name of Producer) all of the Rights;

(b) No motion picture or television or other version or adaptation of the Property has heretofore been produced, performed or copyrighted anywhere in the world;

(c) The Writer will not assign or license, and heretofore the Writer has not assigned or licensed, to any other person, firm or corporation, or in any manner encumbered any of the rights in and to the Property, or any element(s) thereof, granted to Purchaser herein, including the title of the Property, and there are no rights, licenses and/or grants of any kind relating to the Property in favor of any third party. There are no claims, litigation, or other proceedings pending or threatened, which could impair, limit, diminish or infringe upon the Rights;

(d) The Property is wholly original with the Writer, and no incident therein or part thereof is taken from, based upon or adapted from any other literary material, dramatic work, motion picture, television production or other creative dramatic work; and

(e) The Writer hereby waives all "moral rights" (*i.e.* "Droit Moral," as such term is commonly understood throughout the world) with respect to the Rights.

Writer shall indemnify (Name of Producer), its subsidiaries and affiliates, and its and their directors, officers, employees, heirs and assigns (the "Indemnified Parties"), against any and all losses, damages, costs and expenses (including reasonable legal fees) which any or all of the Indemnified Parties may suffer or incur by reason of any breach of any of the representations and warranties made above by Writer.

Writer acknowledges and agrees that, in connection with the Rights, Purchaser shall have the right, but not the obligation, to use, publish and advertise, in any manner or medium it may deem advisable, the name and likeness of (Name of Writer) as author of the Property.

IN WITNESS WHEREOF, the undersigned have executed this instrument this _____ day of _____,
_____.

PRODUCER

Per:_____

_____

Witness

(Name of Writer)

Acknowledgments

Thanks to my brilliant editor, Marjorie Lamb, for her meticulous improvements in the text. If you're writing your novel before you do the screenplay, check out her web site: **http://tinyurl.com/MarjorieLamb** for editing and/or formatting help. E-mail Marjorie at writerinres@gmail.com.

Thanks to filmmaker Peter Rowe for excellent feedback on improving this book. See his web site Peter Rowe Productions Inc. at **http://www.peterrowe.tv/** Also thanks to author Demetrius Sherman for his Q and A with me on the topic of the Sherlock Holmes copyright issues. See his book The Inventors game at **http://tinyurl.com/ShermanBook**

About the author

I'm a writer/producer in the film and television business. My producer credits include the 2009 two-hour Miniseries *Iron Road (see website at www.ironroadthemovie)* an international co-production with China, starring Peter O'Toole, Sam Neill, Sun Li, and Tony Leung Ka Fai. The series has aired on television around the world, and has been released theatrically in 2009 and 2012.

Other feature films: *Isaac Littlefeathers*, starring Lou Jacobi and Scott Hylands; *Alien Warrior*, (Lion's Gate Films); *Plague*, starring Daniel Pilon, Kate Reid and Celine Lomez, which won Best Screenplay and Best Sci-Fi Feature awards at the International Film Festival in Spain.

I also produced the television movies: *Rin-Tin-Tin and the Paris Conspiracy*; *Covert Action*, starring Wendy Crewson and Art Hindle; *The Life and Times of Edwin Alonzo Boyd*, starring Gordon Pinsent; *Crossbar*, starring Kim Cattrall, Brent Carver, and John Ireland.

I have produced more than 300 episodes of television drama, including 13 episodes of *Deepwater Black*, and 106 episodes of *Katts & Dog* (*Rin-Tin-Tin, K-9 Cop* in the U.S.).

My feature film writing credits include: *Paperback Hero*, starring Keir Dullea and Elizabeth Ashley; *Sally Fieldgood & Co.*; *Plague*; *Bloody Birthday*, starring Susan Strasberg and Jose Ferrer; *Firebird 2015 AD*; *Isaac Littlefeathers*; and *Alien Warrior*.

Among my awards are Best Screenplay, Best Picture, at the International Film &Television Festival of New York for *The Life and Times of Edwin Alonzo Boyd*. Best Screenplay, Feature Film, at the 12th International Film Festival in Sitges, Spain for *Plague* and a Special Jury Award, Feature Film at the San Francisco International Film Festival for *Plague*.

Index